MYSTERIES UNWRAPPED:
THE SECRETS OF ALCATRAZ

WRITTEN BY
SUSAN SLOATE

ILLUSTRATED BY
JOSH COCHRAN

STERLING

New York / London
www.sterlingpublishing.com/kids

STERLING and the distinctive Sterling logo are registered trademarks of
Sterling Publishing Co., Inc.

Library of Congress Cataloging-in-Publication Data

Sloate, Susan.
  Mysteries unwrapped: the secrets of Alcatraz / Susan Sloate ; illustrated by Josh Cochran.
     p. cm.
  Includes bibliographical references.
  ISBN-13: 978-1-4027-3591-2
  ISBN-10: 1-4027-3591-X
  1. United States Penitentiary, Alcatraz Island, California—History. 2. Prisons—California—Alcatraz
Island—History. 3. Alcatraz Island (Calif.)—History. I. Cochran, Josh. II. Title.

HV9474.A53S56 2008
365'.979461--dc22

                    2007041123

10 9 8 7 6 5 4 3 2 1

Published by Sterling Publishing Co., Inc.
387 Park Avenue South, New York, NY 10016

Text © 2008 by Susan Sloate
Illustrations © 2008 by Josh Cochran
Distributed in Canada by Sterling Publishing
^c/o Canadian Manda Group, 165 Dufferin Street
Toronto, Ontario, Canada M6K 3H6
Distributed in the United Kingdom by GMC Distribution Services
Castle Place, 166 High Street, Lewes, East Sussex, England BN7 1XU
Distributed in Australia by Capricorn Link (Australia) Pty. Ltd.
P.O. Box 704, Windsor, NSW 2756, Australia

Printed in China

Sterling ISBN-13: 978-1-4027-3591-2
        ISBN-10: 1-4027-3591-X

Book design by Joshua Moore of beardandglasses.com

For information about custom editions, special sales, premium and
corporate purchases, please contact Sterling Special Sales
Department at 800-805-5489 or specialsales@sterlingpublishing.com.

"WELL, WARDEN. IT LOOKS LIKE ALCATRAZ HAS GOT ME LICKED."—AL CAPONE

CONTENTS

PREFACE

The night air was cool, and the wind was blowing briskly over the San Francisco Bay. Even though it was June and much of the country was enjoying a warm summer, the weather here was cold and bleak. At ten o'clock, it was completely dark outside except for the searchlights that flashed from the guard tower every few minutes. From the water came the cry of seagulls.

Inside, it was dark, too. By the warden's order, the lights went out at nine o'clock every night. The only sounds now were the usual ones of men snoring or shifting on their hard cots, trying to find a comfortable position in which to sleep.

In the darkness, four men tensed inside their individual cells, waiting. They had been waiting for months, working for months. At last, tonight, Frank Lee Morris, Allen West, and the brothers John and Clarence Anglin would get away from the Rock . . .

When most people hear the name "Alcatraz," the first thing they think of is the escape-proof prison that served as a last resort for the toughest criminals in America. Although many people find the twenty-nine years when the prison ruled the island the most fascinating part of its history, the small island has served a number of other purposes over the years. Since its discovery in 1775, Alcatraz has housed not only the famous prison but also a fortress to protect the western United States from invasion and a military prison for use during the Civil War. In the 1960s, it became a symbol of defiance for Native Americans, who overran the island and refused to leave for nearly two years.

Today Alcatraz is a national park, open to all those who wish to tour it and learn about the famous convicts who once called it home and the equally famous attempts to escape from the Rock. But in spite of the excitement that Alcatraz now inspires, this small island actually had a very humble beginning.

1.

ALCATRAZ'S BEGINNINGS

FOUNDING OF THE ISLAND

When the Spanish explorer Don Juan Manuel de Ayala sailed into the San Francisco Bay in August 1775, he discovered a series of previously unknown and untouched islands. Among them was a piece of land that seemed to be no more than a blob of barren dirt. There was almost no vegetation and little sign of life beyond the seabirds that momentarily touched down on its shallow shores and then flew off with harsh cries.

De Ayala tried to think of a romantic name for the little bit of land surrounded on all sides by inhospitable cold water, but he was stuck. There was nothing of beauty that he could use as a name. Finally, hearing the seabirds calling, he decided to call it "*La Isla de los Alcatraces*," The Island of the Pelicans. Like others who would come after him, De Ayala found the island distasteful. In fact, he disliked it so much that he never landed on it.

PROTECTION FOR THE WEST

In 1847 California became a territory of the United States. By the time that occurred, cries of "Gold!" had brought eager miners from around the world to the Bay Area to seek fortunes.

The famous Gold Rush increased San Francisco's population by many thousands in just a few years. It also drew the attention of larger countries, such as Japan and Russia, which at that time were more powerful than the United States. Those countries realized how rich the land of America's west coast actually was and how easily they might acquire it. Worried that more powerful nations would try to seize American land, the U.S. Army decided to establish a military presence there, and to do so quickly. After much consideration, the government settled on that the tiny island in the middle of the bay, whose name had been simplified to Alcatraz, as the perfect spot for a new fortress.

In 1853, construction began on a military fortress. When building was completed a few years later, the Army moved in. The new fortress boasted four 36,000-pound, fifteen-inch Rodman guns—heavy weapons that could fire on and sink hostile ships up to three miles away. The island was also ringed with heavy, long-range cannons on all sides. Altogether, the weapons were capable of firing almost 7,000 pounds of iron shot at once.

That was impressive, but it proved ultimately unnecessary. As a defender of the West Coast, the cannons of Alcatraz fired only a single round—400 pounds of ammunition—and failed to hit the ship they were aiming at. Over the next thirty years, the weaponry that had seemed so impressive when the fortress had been built became obsolete. Furthermore, there did not appear to be any ongoing threat from other countries to the west. There seemed to be little need to house a full-scale army unit permanently on an island where everything—food, water, and all supplies—had to be painstakingly brought in from the mainland.

The army began to reconsider its use for Alcatraz. The factors that were drawbacks in maintaining an army—the freezing water, the long distance from land, and the heavy currents—could be great assets if the fortress was turned into a military prison. Anyone brought to Alcatraz as a prisoner would have almost no chance of leaving the island on his own.

And so the military fortress, never having had to defend its coastline, became a prison.

ALCATRAZ BECOMES A MILITARY PRISON

The first prisoners to set foot on Alcatraz were Confederate soldiers captured during the Civil War. Union soldiers also were imprisoned on Alcatraz for crimes such as disobedience to an officer and desertion. Although the prison could hold hundreds of captives, no more than thirty Civil War prisoners were ever held there at the same time. When the Spanish American War began in 1898, however, the number of prisoners brought to the island rose from 26 to over 450. It was the first time a sizable population of prisoners had been held there, and cells were built wherever there was space, including in the damp, dark, and cold dungeons. The dungeons had been built to hold disobedient soldiers when the island was a fortress, but the military commanders decided they would work fine as permanent cells.

ALCATRAZ BECOMES A LOW-SECURITY PRISON

In 1906, San Francisco experienced a devastating earthquake, which was followed by a fire that raged out of control for days. With the city in chaos and the police and fire departments fully

THE DUNGEONS HAD BEEN
BUILT TO HOLD
DISOBEDIENT SOLDIERS
WHEN THE ISLAND WAS A
FORTRESS, BUT THE
MILITARY COMMANDERS
DECIDED THEY WOULD WORK
FINE AS PERMANENT CELLS.

occupied in restoring order and getting things to run efficiently again, there was no way to protect the citizens of San Francisco against the convicts who were imprisoned in the city's jails.

After much discussion, it was decided that hundreds of civilian prisoners would be brought to Alcatraz. There they were mixed with the soldiers who were serving time on the island. On the basis of their crimes and their behavior in prison, the convicts were divided into three classes. No prisoner was permitted to stay in his cell during the day, but the way the prisoners' time was spent differed greatly with their class ranking.

Prisoners with class one and two rankings were considered the least dangerous and most cooperative. They were guarded less heavily than were inmates at other prisons and were permitted to go anywhere on the island except the guards' quarters. One of the prisoners' favorite details was doing the gardening around the island. Some prisoners worked as servants for the families living on the island, cooking and cleaning in their homes during the day. The most trusted prisoners were even assigned to take care of the staff's children.

Class three prisoners were the most heavily supervised and restricted. They were not allowed off the prison site, could not speak at any time, and could not have letters or visitors, or read material from the prison library.

Prisoners who broke the rules were punished harshly. Their class ranking was lowered immediately, and they commonly received punishments such as solitary confinement, a diet of bread and water, or even wearing a twelve-pound iron ball and chain around their ankles.

By the 1920s, however, the rules had become more relaxed. Prisoners were allowed to build a baseball field on the grounds and wore their own team uniforms instead of prison clothes during the games. Friday night boxing matches also became common and were attended by visitors from the mainland. As military discipline moved toward more modern methods, incorporating more rehabilitation and less harsh punishment, Alcatraz began to reflect a new idea about how a prison should be run.

CHILDREN OF ALCATRAZ

During its time as a federal prison Alcatraz was also home to the wardens and guards, many of whom had children. Although they lived on the same island as the country's most hardened criminals, the families seldom locked their doors, and the children roamed the island freely, exploring and playing, thinking little of the men locked in the prison buildings just a few hundred yards away.

The same ferry that brought new prisoners from the mainland to Alcatraz took the children of Alcatraz back and forth to their mainland schools. There, they were often regarded as celebrities for living on the Rock among famous criminals.

However, the safety they took for granted on the island was not always complete. The children had to abide by plenty of rules, which included not owning bicycles, pets, or toy guns, probably so that the inmates could not use them during an escape attempt. They were also forbidden to go down to the beach, near the cold water and treacherous tides. And during a bloody escape attempt in 1946, the children had to be sheltered on the mainland until the crisis was over.

Today, many of those who grew up on Alcatraz return for an annual reunion. Although they live all over the country, the life they remember and the place where they once lived keep them close.

ALCATRAZ BECOMES A HIGH-SECURITY PRISON

In 1934, the operation of Alcatraz was turned over to the U.S. Department of Justice. The country was in an economic slump called the Great Depression, and the cost of running the island had become too high for the Army.

At the same time, America was experiencing a remarkable wave of violent crime. The Justice Department decided to turn Alcatraz into a maximum-security prison, but first it would have to modify the facility. The criminals sent to Alcatraz would not be the easily controlled nonviolent offenders the island once had housed. They would be the worst of the worst, the toughest, the most difficult, the hardest to control. The Justice Department decided to make Alcatraz the prison of last resort. Only prisoners who could not be controlled at other prisons would be sent there. By the time Alcatraz was ready for its new population, it had become a criminal's worst nightmare.

It eventually would become known as Uncle Sam's Devil's Island. Like the famous French island prison Devil's Island, this American prison was a last-resort prison of the harshest kind, and many prisoners who arrived there left broken in spirit— or dead.

THE TOUGHEST
2. PRISON IN AMERICA

In April 1934, security experts went to work on Alcatraz. The soft cell bars of the Army detention days were replaced with hard steel bars that could not be cut through. Electric lights were installed in every cell, and electricity was used to open and close cell block doors. The cells were arranged so that none adjoined an outside wall. Even if a prisoner somehow got out of his cell, he would still have to find a way to escape from the prison building itself.

To prevent escape from the building, every window in areas that convicts could enter was covered with a sheet of iron. Tear gas canisters that could be activated by remote control were hidden in the ceiling of the dining hall and could be used to subdue prisoners in case of a riot or escape attempt. Electromagnetic detectors were placed all over the island to detect the presence of guns or other weapons hidden on the prisoners' bodies. Special elevated galleries built during the renovation now held twenty-four-hour guards armed with rifles who could see into every cell, and utility tunnels were filled with cement to make it impossible for prisoners to hide in them.

THE RULES OF ALCATRAZ

Although Alcatraz had a total of 600 cells for individual prisoners, as a security measure it never held more than 300 prisoners at any one time. (Other federal prisons, such as Leavenworth, held over 3,500.) The ratio of prisoners to guards on Alcatraz was three to one, lower than at any other prison, and that allowed the guards to keep a much closer watch over the prisoners. In fact, the prison population was so small that the guards knew all the inmates by name. Those 300 prisoners lived under the leadership of Warden James A. Johnston and were expected to abide by the rules he established.

Under Johnston's command, prisoners were not allowed visitors for their first ninety days on the island. Once that time had passed, they were permitted one visitor a month. Other criminals or anyone who might encourage bad behavior among the inmates were not allowed to visit.

The prisoners' knowledge of the outside world was carefully curbed. No newspapers, magazines, or radios were allowed, and the prisoners were given only the barest necessities: food, clothing, medical and dental care, and the meager contents of their cells, which included a sink and a toilet. Everything else was con sidered a privilege and had to be earned by good behavior. All privileges could be revoked immediately if a prisoner broke a rule.

One particularly harsh rule enforced by Johnston in the early years was a strict code of silence. The prisoners considered this the greatest hardship of all. Some, desperate to talk to someone and hear a human voice, emptied the water from the toilets in

James A. Johnston—the toughest warden on Alcatraz.
(© BETTMANN/CORBIS)

THE TOUGHEST PRISON IN AMERICA | 11

INMATES DRIVEN MAD

The regulations and unchanging routine of Alcatraz—especially the forced silence—drove more than one prisoner to desperation. Ed Wutke, Alcatraz prisoner number AZ#I0906, was the first to commit suicide while imprisoned on the island. Over the years there were many more.

Others took extreme measures against the silence, such as the gangster and bank robber Rufe Persful, who was assigned to work in the mat shop, cutting up old rubber tires. One day two years after his imprisonment on the island, Persful—supposedly driven mad by the unending silence—took a hatchet and chopped off the fingers on one of his hands. He then held out the hatchet to the inmate next to him and told him to chop off the fingers on his other hand. Persful was taken to the hospital wing before the inmate could oblige.

A few years later the policy of silence was relaxed, and inmates were permitted to talk. By the I950s, they were also allowed to keep books and radios, subscribe to certain magazines, see movies twice a month, attend religious services inside the prison, and play musical instruments.

their cells and spoke into the bowls. The effect was an echo in the next inmate's cell, which allowed prisoners to converse in whispers.

In other prisons, wealthy and influential convicts could bribe their way to a comfortable lifestyle behind bars. In fact, some lived as well in prison as out of it, finding that with enough money, the rules did not apply to them. In Alcatraz that was impossible. No one got special privileges, not even the most famous criminals. Activities were too well monitored, and the small number of prisoners on the island ensured that they were all treated the same. The warden even kept a filing-card system on which he noted information about each individual prisoner for a prisoner's entire stay on the island.

THE PRISONERS ARRIVE ON ALCATRAZ

In August 1934, Alcatraz began to receive civilian prisoners from around the country. In just a few weeks there were 166 new convicts on the island. Each prisoner arrived chained at the wrists and ankles. The inmates were driven to the prison building and processed by several guards before coming face to face with the warden, who greeted every new "fish"—or prisoner—personally. The inmates were allowed to take a brief shower and were then taken to their cells, walking down the long corridor the convicts called Broadway because it was the busiest hallway in the prison cell block. There they were given a handbook to read, outlining the rules of the island.

Then the cell door slammed shut.

The right to work was the first privilege the inmates could earn, and it was important. It meant that a convict could leave his cell during the day and have something to occupy his mind. Without a job, a prisoner spent his entire waking time—except for meals and a period in the exercise yard—alone in his five- by eight-foot cell, in which a man standing in the middle and extending his arms could easily touch each wall. Remaining in the cell quickly grew unbearable. Having a job at least helped relieve the boredom.

Prisoners could work in several areas of the main building, including the laundry, the kitchens, the tailor shop, and the prison library, or they could work on the dock or in the industries building, which made items such as clothing under government contract. The inmates earned a small hourly wage, which was placed in a personal account that they received when they left the island. In spite of their ability to work in several prison locations, the convicts' time on Alcatraz was so well monitored that the inmates never had a chance to see the entire prison building, only the few areas they were permitted to enter.

Restricting convicts' access to the prison was intended to keep them from making escape plans. If they didn't know the entire layout of the prison and the island, it would be more difficult to plan an escape. The tight security also helped maintain discipline among the inmates.

Even in Alcatraz, however, there were inmates who refused to play by the rules. When that happened, the prisoners were placed in cell block D—solitary confinement.

SOLITARY CONFINEMENT

There were three basic types of solitary confinement in Alcatraz. The first and least restrictive was given for breaking minor rules such as consistently being late for head count. The confinement was carried out in a group of thirty-six cells that kept prisoners isolated for long periods but gave them a chance to have two showers a week and one visit a week to the recreation yard. For the rest of the time, they remained in their cells, even eating their meals there. From their upper-tier windows, they could see San Francisco; that view could be maddening, as it gave them a glimpse of the freedom they might never have.

SOME INMATES WERE
EVEN MORE DIFFICULT....
THEIR PUNISHMENT WAS
THE HARSHEST OF ALL.
THOSE PRISONERS WERE
SENT TO THE STRIP CELL,
SOMETIMES CALLED THE
ORIENTAL, FOR PERIODS OF
UP TO TWO DAYS. THAT WAS
ALL EVEN THE TOUGHEST
CONS COULD HANDLE.

The second method of confinement was a special block of five double-doored cells called the Hole where prisoners could be confined for up to nineteen days at a time. Prisoners never left their cells during that period, and each cell contained nothing but a toilet, a sink, and a lightbulb. The mattresses they slept on were removed during the day, leaving the prisoners with nothing to do. The boredom was terrible. Occasionally guards would open the window in the outer door to let in light for a few minutes for convicts who were serving their time quietly.

Some inmates were even more difficult. They didn't just talk out of turn or fail to keep their cells clean. They assaulted other prisoners or guards or tried to escape. Their punishment was the harshest of all. Those prisoners were sent to the Strip Cell, sometimes called the Oriental, for periods of up to two days. That was all even the toughest cons could handle.

The Strip Cell was encased in steel and kept dark day and night. Prisoners were locked naked and alone in a completely bare cell, with no sink and just a hole in the floor to serve as a toilet. The mattress they slept on at night was taken away during the day, and the cell was kept cold. Their diet consisted of water and four slices of bread a day. They saw no one except the guard, who shoved food into the cell three times a day but was forbidden to speak to them. The rest of the time an inmate was left to himself in complete darkness.

Everyone feared the Strip Cell—even the biggest braggarts and the most violent offenders. Life in the regular population at Alcatraz was barely tolerable, and solitary confinement could be endured if necessary, but spending time in the Strip Cell unnerved them all.

But for the public, it is not the wardens, the restrictive rules, or even how the prisoners were punished that is so fascinating. It's the famous prisoners ...

Alcatraz's solitary confinement cells, where prisoners who broke the rules could spend days, weeks, or even months. (© BETTMANN/CORBIS)

3. FAMOUS PRISONERS

Over the twenty nine years that it served as a federal prison, Alcatraz played host to a number of well-known inmates. Some of them were famous when they arrived on Alcatraz; they were the criminals J. Edgar Hoover, the director of the Federal Bureau of Investigation (FBI), had described as "public enemies," and their faces and crimes were known from wanted posters and newspaper reports. Others became famous only for being imprisoned on the Rock. They were bank robbers, bootleggers, and murderers, and they were considered too dangerous to be kept in other prisons.

AL CAPONE

Perhaps the most famous prisoner ever to stay on Alcatraz was the Chicago gangster Al Capone. Capone was a high-living, fast-talking mobster who ran the Chicago crime scene. He was involved in every sort of illegal activity, from gambling to liquor to drugs. His empire stretched across the country but mostly was centered in the Midwest, where he lived. It was said that in 1929 he was worth $62 million, which would be over $700 million today. His share of the businesses he was involved with brought in about $100,000 a week.

WITH THE LARGE SUMS OF MONEY HE KEPT HIDDEN IN HIS CELL, CAPONE BRIBED THE PRISON GUARDS TO HELP HIM RUN HIS BUSINESS EMPIRE FROM BEHIND BARS. HE WAS ALSO GIVEN UNLIMITED ACCESS TO THE PRISON WARDEN, SOMETHING NO OTHER PRISONER WAS PERMITTED. FOR CAPONE, THE RULES DIDN'T APPLY.

Capone committed all kinds of crimes, including murder, but was never convicted of any of them because he bribed politicians, judges, and the police to look the other way when he did something illegal. In the end, it was the Treasury Department that finally discovered a way to nail Capone. Instead of trying to catch him for his violent crimes, they arrested him for not paying income tax. In October 1931 Capone was finally sentenced to eleven years in jail for the nonviolent crime of cheating the Internal Revenue Service.

Capone spent the first seven months of his sentence in the Cook County Jail in Illinois, which was right in the heart of his

Al Capone—Alcatraz's most famous prisoner. (© BETTMANN/CORBIS)

stomping grounds. Even in prison, he remained powerful and influential. He had a constant stream of visitors and continued to run his businesses without interference.

In May 1932, he was transferred to Atlanta. With the large sums of money he kept hidden in his cell, Capone bribed the prison guards to help him run his business empire from behind bars. He was also given unlimited access to the prison warden, something no other prisoner was permitted. For Capone, the rules didn't apply.

Eventually, U.S. Attorney General Homer Cummings became fed up with Capone's highhandedness. Capone's belief that he was above the law was creating a serious disciplinary problem. Cummings and Sanford Bates, the head of the federal prison system, quietly worked to transfer Capone to Alcatraz. Suddenly, Capone was subjected to the same tough discipline as everyone else.

Capone arrived on Alcatraz in August in the first batch of prisoners transferred from Atlanta. His stay on Alcatraz took place during its harshest period. On meeting Warden Johnston and the other new fish, he immediately tried to assume the role of leader. He wanted the other prisoners to know that even there they could count on him to "fix" things for them.

Johnston was not impressed with Capone's big talk. He gave him a prison number—AZ#85—and told the mobster that he would obey Alcatraz's rules, just like any other convict.

Surprisingly, Capone did. He was given none of the privileges he had enjoyed at Cook County and Atlanta. Like the other prisoners, he was isolated completely from the outside world for his first ninety days, and after that his access to mail, visitors, and news was severely limited. Although he tried several times to persuade the warden to give him special privileges, Johnston never budged. What was fair for one prisoner was fair for another, even one as famous as Al Capone.

Eventually, Capone gave up trying to move the warden. He submitted to Alcatraz's iron discipline and spent his time sweeping floors in the cell house—a job probably designed to humble him. Later he worked in the boot repair shop, where he learned to be an excellent cobbler. He no longer tried to bribe the guards and kept his bare cell as clean as those of the other inmates. In exchange for his good behavior, he was permitted to play the banjo, a skill he had learned outside prison, and soon joined a four-man prison band.

But Capone's four and a half years on Alcatraz were not unblemished. He fought with another prisoner and was put into second-degree isolation for eight days as punishment. Later, while working in the prison basement, he got into a brawl with an inmate who was waiting in line for a haircut. They shouted at each other, and the convict stabbed Capone with a pair of scissors. Capone ended up in the prison hospital with a minor wound and returned to his cell a few days later.

Over the years, whether because of his time on Alcatraz or because of a disease that ravaged his mind, Capone began to exhibit strange behavior. He sometimes refused to leave his cell and spent his time crouched on the floor, babbling to himself and playing the banjo. After a while, he became afraid to go into the recreation yard with the other prisoners and hid in the shower room instead. Sometimes he was even seen making his bunk again and again and talking baby talk.

In late 1938, Capone was transferred to Terminal Island in southern California, where he served out the rest of his sentence. He was finally released in November 1939, but by then he was on the verge of complete insanity. He died of his longtime disease in January 1947 in his lavish Palm Island home.

Capone's wry comment to Warden James Johnston early in his stay at Alcatraz summed up the toughness of his life on the Rock. "Well, Warden," he said, "it looks like Alcatraz has got me licked."

"MACHINE GUN" KELLY

Although George "Machine Gun" Kelly was as colorful a character as Capone in the public's mind, his life and stay on Alcatraz were entirely different.

Born George Kelly Barnes, he came from a wealthy family, and his upbringing was normal and uneventful. Kelly's life took a turn for the worse, however, when he met and married Geneva Ramsey, with whom he had two children. Money was tight, and Kelly turned to selling illegal liquor to support his family.

After being arrested and imprisoned for his crimes several times, Kelly decided to leave home, abandoning his wife and children. Eventually he met Kathryn Thorne, the girlfriend of one of his associates and a tough criminal in her own right. Kathryn's influence on the small-time criminal soon turned him into public enemy number one on J. Edgar Hoover's most wanted list. She bought Kelly a machine gun and urged him to practice with it. Soon Kelly turned to robbing banks, always taking the machine gun with him. The ensuing publicity, which Kathryn loved, made him known as Machine Gun Kelly.

Armed guards escort George "Machine Gun" Kelly out of a Memphis jail.
(© BETTMANN/CORBIS)

George "Machine Gun" Kelly and Kathryn Thorne on trial for the kidnapping of Charles Urschel (© BETTMANN/CORBIS)

Kelly and Kathryn were married in September 1930, and together they lived high, running from one bank robbery to another. Kathryn, always promoting her husband's image, was said to carry spent gun cartridges with her and drop them in front of people during a casual conversation, telling them the cartridges were souvenirs from Kelly's famous machine gun (known at that time as a tommy gun).

In July 1933, Kelly, Kathryn, and two accomplices kidnapped a wealthy oil tycoon named Charles Urschel and tried to ransom him for $200,000. The money was delivered, and Urschel was released unharmed after eight days in captivity. But the kidnappers had overlooked the tycoon's cool head and determination to help the law. During the time he was held, Urschel made certain to leave his fingerprints everywhere he could and to remember sounds and count steps whenever he walked from one place to another.

On September 26, FBI agents surrounded the home of a friend who was sheltering the kidnappers. The agents burst in, surprising Kelly, who was still in his pajamas, and Kathryn, who was in bed asleep.

Kelly threw up his hands and said, "G-men, please don't shoot!" a phrase that has become famous. He and Kathryn were taken into custody, and Kelly was sentenced to life in prison at Leavenworth Penitentiary.

Once there, he began to taunt prison officials. He told them he would break out of Leavenworth and then bust his wife out of her prison. Prison officials had seen the FBI posters of Machine Gun Kelly and took him seriously. They felt he was perfectly capable of doing what he said. After much consultation, they decided the best thing to do was to remove him from Leavenworth altogether.

Kelly arrived at Alcatraz in September 1934. He was assigned prison number AZ#117 and settled into a cell on the second tier of block B.

Even on Alcatraz he remained a braggart who constantly told others tall tales about his escapades as a bank robber and murderer—although there is no evidence that he ever murdered anyone. The men who worked with him in his prison industries job knew his reputation as public enemy number one, but they dismissed his stories as big talk. One of the men did claim, however, that Kelly used to accuse him of snoring and hit his head with a magazine every night to stop it.

Unlike Al Capone, Machine Gun Kelly was what Warden Johnston considered a model prisoner. He worked every day, first in the prison laundry and then in an administrative job in the prison industries, and was generally quiet and gave the guards no trouble. He even became an altar boy at the prison chapel and went to religious services regularly. Like Capone, he joined the prison band, playing the drums. Kelly wrote as many letters as he was allowed, though the letters he received from his family seemed to make him unhappy. He showed remorse for his crimes but also believed that Kathryn and the other members of his gang had been treated worse than they deserved. He even sent several letters to the man he had kidnapped and held for ransom, apologizing for the kidnapping and asking if Urschel would speak to judges and other authorities on his behalf. Urschel never replied.

Kelly spent seventeen years on the Rock before being transferred back to Leavenworth, where he died of a heart attack on his fifty-ninth birthday in July 1954. His wife, Kathryn, who did so much to promote his image as a violent gangster, became a bookkeeper at an Oklahoma hospital after she was released from prison in 1958.

THE BIRDMAN OF ALCATRAZ

Unlike Al Capone and Machine Gun Kelly, who were well known before their years in prison, Robert Stroud—the Birdman of Alcatraz—became famous only after he had begun to serve his time.

Stroud was a career criminal who started on the wrong road early in life. In 1909, at the age of nineteen, he murdered a bartender over ten dollars Stroud thought was owed to him. He was convicted of manslaughter in 1911 and sentenced to twelve years in McNeil Penitentiary in Washington, where he distinguished himself by various outbursts of violence, including assaulting a prison hospital orderly and stabbing another inmate.

Stroud's violent actions in McNeil earned him not only six additional months in jail but also a transfer in 1912 to Leavenworth, a new maximum-security prison. At Leavenworth he was allowed to take courses in subjects such as astronomy and structural engineering and excelled at them even though he had only a third grade education. He also studied theosophy, a form of religion that combines spirituality with science and philosophy, and seemed to get comfort from it. In 1915 he was diagnosed with Bright's disease, an incurable illness that causes an inflammation of the kidneys and constant pain. He grew thinner and weaker and feared he would never see his family again. Most of his time was spent in the prison's hospital wing.

Eventually, he became stronger and was returned to his prison cell, but the pain and weakness had changed him. He gave up his studies and his spiritual beliefs and grew bitter and angry. It did not help that one of the new prison guards, Andrew F.

THE TURNING POINT IN STROUD'S LIFE CAME WHEN HE FOUND AN INJURED CANARY DURING ONE OF HIS SOLITARY PERIODS IN THE PRISON RECREATION YARD. HE WAS ALLOWED TO NURSE IT, AND HIS FASCINATION WITH BIRDS AND THEIR DISEASES BEGAN.

Robert Stroud—the Birdman of Alcatraz. (© BETTMANN/CORBIS)

Turner, enjoyed taunting and threatening the prisoners. In 1916, Stroud learned that his brother Marcus had come to fulfill a long-planned visit to him and had been turned away by prison officials. Stroud was angry about it and complained to another prisoner, breaking the prison's rule of silence. Turner overheard him and reported him, which cost Stroud further visiting privileges. Furious, Stroud stabbed Turner to death in full view of eleven hundred prisoners in the mess hall. He was convicted of first-degree murder and sentenced to death by hanging, but Stroud's mother pleaded with President Woodrow Wilson to spare her son. In 1920, the President agreed to alter the sentence to life imprisonment without parole.

Stroud would never walk free again.

But the warden at Leavenworth had had enough of Stroud's violent nature. He directed his officers to place Stroud in permanent segregation so that he could never again threaten an inmate or guard. Stroud would remain in isolation at Leavenworth for more than twenty-two years.

The turning point in Stroud's life came when he found an injured canary during one of his solitary periods in the prison recreation yard. He was allowed to nurse it, and his fascination with birds and their diseases began.

Stroud started to study birds carefully. With the warden's permission, he built a laboratory in two segregation cells that stood side by side. The warden hoped that allowing Stroud to do something productive would occupy his time and reduce his violent urges, which it did seem to do. Stroud conducted experiments on the birds, bred them, nursed them, and studied their diseases. He sold the canaries he raised to prison visitors. At one point, FBI director J. Edgar Hoover even bought a canary from him!

Stroud wrote two books on canaries and their diseases and developed medicines for those diseases that he marketed outside the prison with the help of a sympathetic bird lover who later became his wife.

Eventually, however, the guards discovered that some of the equipment Stroud had in his lab was being used not for bird research but to make homemade alcohol. The warden ordered the lab shut down. At the same time, outside groups concerned with wildlife were making life miserable for the warden and staff at Leavenworth. They were demanding special treatment for Stroud on the basis of his bird work, unaware of or uninterested in the fact that he was still a violent and dangerous prisoner.

Stroud, too, was demanding and difficult. Besides brewing his own alcohol, he had so many birds in his cell that it was filthy and unsanitary. There were bird droppings everywhere as well as the bodies of birds he was dissecting for scientific research. Finally the warden decided that he had had enough of Robert Stroud. In 1942 he sent Stroud to Alcatraz, where he became prisoner AZ#594.

Stroud is the only prisoner who ever spent his entire time on the Rock isolated from all the other prisoners. He was never put into a cell in the general population because prison officials feared his violent nature. His first six years were spent in D block—solitary confinement. For the next eleven years, he had a cell in the prison hospital, partly because he was often ill and required medical treatment but also to separate him even more from the other prisoners. He was not allowed in the mess hall and was seldom permitted to use the recreation yard. Occasionally he was allowed to play a game of chess with one of his guards, but that was all the social interaction he had. He spent his time reading and studying and apparently learned a number of languages.

By the time Stroud reached Alcatraz, he had been behind bars for twenty-five years and believed he had served enough time. He studied prison library books about the legal system, trying to arrange his release from prison through a stream of petitions for a pardon. He felt that he had paid his debt to society and deserved to be freed. But every time he asked for his release, it was denied.

Despite his famous nickname, Stroud was never allowed to raise or study live birds on Alcatraz, although he was permitted to continue his studies by reading journals and books about birds.

In 1959, he was sent to the Medical Center for Federal Prisoners in Springfield, Missouri. He stayed there until his death in November 1963 at the age of seventy-three.

HENRY "HENRI" YOUNG

In 1939, Henry Young joined four other prisoners in an escape attempt that ended with one prisoner being shot to death. Young and the others were recaptured and put in low-level isolation cells, although Young apparently returned to the general population by the fall of that year. In December 1940, after the 10 A.M. head count in the industries building, Young hurried upstairs to the furniture shop where Rufus McCain, one of his fellow escapees, was working and stabbed him to death.

Young was tried for murder in San Francisco, and his trial became the first source of information the general public had about conditions at Alcatraz. Much of it was misleading information, and some was downright wrong. Yet it led to a wave of stories and even movies about life on the Rock.

Prisoners testified about the unending silence, the isolation, and the routine. Some even mentioned rumors about prisoners in dungeons being beaten by guards. Prisoners were said to have been driven crazy and led off the island in straitjackets. None of it was true.

However, those statements accomplished what Young's attorneys hoped for. Since their client had committed murder in front of witnesses, they could not argue that he had not done it. Instead, they had to "prove" that it was the conditions of Alcatraz, not their client's violent nature, that had led to McCain's death.

The strategy worked. The jury was sympathetic, believing many of the lies the prisoners told. In April 1941 they convicted Young of involuntary manslaughter. He was sentenced to life imprisonment for the crime and remained at Alcatraz until 1948, when he was sent to the Medical Center for Federal Prisoners in Springfield, Missouri. When his federal sentence was up in 1954, he was sent to the Washington State Penitentiary in Walla Walla to serve a life sentence for a murder committed years earlier.

In 1972 he was released from the penitentiary. As a condition of his parole, he was required to let prison authorities know where he was at all times. Yet soon afterward he vanished. The authorities have no information on him and no idea, even today, whether he is alive or dead.

ATTEMPTED ESCAPES

4.

As Henry Young and his fellow prisoners proved, escape from Alcatraz was unlikely. The island was over a mile from the mainland, and it was all but impossible to swim the bay without being dragged down and drowned by the currents or quickly incapacitated by the cold temperature of the water, which remained between forty-eight and fifty-four degrees all year long. Although some well-conditioned swimmers had done the swim from San Francisco to Alcatraz as a stunt, the warden made sure that his prisoners were never conditioned enough to attempt it. To keep them from getting used to the cold waters of the bay, which might help them survive the swim, the warden made sure the prisoners' showers were always comfortably hot. In addition, the prisoners were never permitted enough rigorous exercise to get in shape to swim the bay. In the twenty-nine years that Alcatraz operated as a federal prison, there were only fourteen escape attempts, involving thirty-four different inmates. (Two of them actually tried to escape twice!) In those thirty-six total attempts, twenty-three prisoners were recaptured almost at once. Two drowned, and six were shot and killed. The records list the remaining five as "missing, presumed drowned."

All but one escape attempt ended in complete failure. Some were clever, and some were violent. There were single prisoner attempts and multiple prisoner attempts. But what all of them had in common was the desperation of the men who planned and executed them. Those men would do anything to get away from the Rock.

APRIL 27, 1936

The first attempt to escape from the island was in 1936, two years after Alcatraz opened as a federal prison. Joe Bowers, who worked at the incinerator burning trash, climbed a chain-link fence at the water's edge. A guard shouted at him to stop, but Bowers paid no attention and scurried frantically up the fence. He was shot, fell almost a hundred feet, and died.

DECEMBER 16, 1937

In 1937, Theodore Cole and Ralph Roe, two prisoners working in one of the prison shops, patiently filed down the iron bars on the windows with shop tools. They then escaped through the windows and made their way down to the bay. However, the weather was bad and the currents in the water were strong. Both men disappeared; their bodies were never recovered, nor did they ever reappear on land. After an extensive search, prison officials listed them as "missing, presumed drowned."

MAY 23, 1938

In May 1938, three prisoners in the woodworking shop attacked and killed an unarmed corrections officer named Royal Cline and then climbed into the guard tower to attack a second guard—Harold Stites—who shot two of the prisoners, James

Limerick and Rufus Franklin. The shooting quickly ended the escape attempt. Limerick died of his injuries, while Franklin, who survived the shooting, and Jimmy Lucas, the third prisoner, were sentenced to life in prison for Cline's murder.

JANUARY 13, 1939

In 1939, Arthur "Doc" Barker and four other prisoners—Henry Young, Rufus McCain, Dale Stamphill, and William Martin—escaped from the isolation unit by sawing through the bars on the windows and got to the shore on the western side of Alcatraz. There they ran into guards who ordered them to surrender. Three did, and these men were taken into custody. Stamphill and Barker refused to give up, and they were shot. Barker died in the shooting, and the surviving escapees were sent back to isolation.

MAY 2, 1941

In May 1941, four inmates—Lloyd Barkdoll, Joe Cretzer, Sam Shockley, and Arnold Kyle—took several officers hostage and attempted to shoot their way out of Alcatraz. One of the hostages, Paul Madigan—who eventually would become the third warden on the island—somehow persuaded the men that they could not pull off the escape, the men surrendered and were placed in isolation.

SEPTEMBER 15, 1941

In September 1941, John Bayless, an inmate working on garbage detail, got down to the bay without being stopped. However, he could not stand the cold water and decided to go back.

APRIL 14, 1943

In April 1943, four prisoners—James Boarman, Harold Brest, Fred Hunter, and Floyd Hamilton—took two guards hostage in the industries building during the workday. The inmates climbed out a window and got down to the shore with the hostages, one of whom was able to signal to other guards, who began firing. Boarman was shot and sank into the bay. Though his body was not recovered, he was presumed dead. Brest and Hunter were captured immediately. Initially, Hamilton was thought to have gotten away. In reality, he had hidden in a cave on one side of the island, but after almost drowning during high tide, he made his way back to the place where he had made his escape. He was found, battered and bruised, two days later.

AUGUST 7, 1943

In August 1943, Huron "Ted" Walters, an inmate in the laundry facility, managed to get out and down to the shore. He was recaptured before he could set foot in the water.

JULY 31, 1945

In July of 1945, inmate John Giles attempted one of the cleverest escapes in Alcatraz's history. Giles worked at the loading dock, where he regularly unloaded army uniforms that had been sent to the island's dry-cleaning plant. Over a period of months, he quietly stole bits and pieces of various uniforms until he had assembled an entire outfit. Then he simply put it on and stepped aboard the launch that was leaving Alcatraz.

Because of the constant head counts, Giles's absence was noticed almost at once. The alarm sounded all over the island, and guards were immediately on the alert.

To make matters worse, Giles thought that the launch was headed for the mainland. It was not; it was going to nearby Angel Island. When the launch reached Angel Island, correctional officers nabbed Giles and returned him to Alcatraz.

MAY 2-4, 1946: THE BATTLE OF ALCATRAZ

The bloodiest escape attempt—although ultimately unsuccessful—took place in May 1946 and became known as the Battle of Alcatraz. Six inmates—including Joe Cretzer and Sam Shockley, who had attempted to escape with a group of others in 1941—subdued nine guards, threw them into two cells, and took possession of both their weapons and the keys to the cell block. Unfortunately for them, the key that opened the door to the recreation yard was not there. One of the officers who was being held hostage had the key, but he refused to tell the frantic inmates where it was. When they were not looking at him, he hid it in the toilet of the cell where he was imprisoned. Meanwhile, other prison officials discovered the disturbance and set off sirens all over the island, mobilizing the entire staff.

As guards swarmed toward their position, Joe Cretzer aimed his revolver at the helpless guards locked in cell number 403 and began firing at point-blank range. One guard, Harold Stites—who had foiled an earlier escape attempt—charged toward the inmates, returning fire. He was cut down and was the first to be pronounced dead. A second guard, William Miller—the guard who had hidden the yard key and refused to say where it was—died from his injuries. A number of others were wounded.

The associate warden took fourteen men to the cell block in an attempt to put an end to the hostage situation, but he and his men met with heavy fire from the inmates and had to retreat.

Meanwhile, the U.S. Marines had shown up to help. They poured in explosives, tear gas, and hand grenades from the roof. A number of prisoners who were locked in their cells were caught in the smoke, choking and unable to escape from the explosions. They tried to soak their mattresses with water from their sinks and toilets and hide behind them to protect themselves from the gas, but it did little good. They were locked in, unarmed and in the middle of a major battle.

In addition to the smoke, the explosives used by the Marines had damaged the water pipes in D block. Water flooded into the cell block as explosives and grenades continued to blow up.

Suddenly, Robert Stroud—the Birdman of Alcatraz—appeared in the middle of the chaos. He climbed down from the third tier in D block, where he was being housed, to the bottom floor. He had been left unguarded when his personal guards had joined the gun battle. Stroud ran along the row of isolation cells, closing the cell doors in an attempt to shield the prisoners from the gunfire, and called up to one of the warden's lieutenants that the inmates responsible were no longer in the cell block.

After forty-eight straight hours of chaos and gun fighting, Alcatraz finally became quiet.

The warden's men had successfully captured Sam Shockley, Miran Thompson, and Clarence Carnes. Two guards were dead,

STROUD RAN ALONG THE ROW OF ISOLATION CELLS, CLOSING THE CELL DOORS IN AN ATTEMPT TO SHIELD THE PRISONERS FROM THE GUNFIRE, AND CALLED UP TO ONE OF THE WARDEN'S LIEUTENANTS THAT THE INMATES RESPONSIBLE WERE NO LONGER IN THE CELL BLOCK.

and eighteen others had been injured. Two days later, the bodies of Bernard Coy, Joe Cretzer, and Marvin Hubbard were found together in a utility corridor, where they had clearly been trying to hide. They were riddled with bullet holes. Coy was wearing a guard's uniform, which he had intended to use to disguise himself. Cretzer still cradled the gun he had used to fire at the guards.

The remaining inmates—Shockley, Thompson, and Carnes— were tried for the murder of the two guards and were convicted. Shockley and Thompson were sentenced to die in the gas chamber at San Quentin Prison. Carnes, who at age nineteen was the youngest prisoner Alcatraz had ever had, was spared the gas chamber because of his youth. Instead, he was given an additional ninety-nine-year sentence. He would never leave prison.

JULY 23, 1956

In 1956, Floyd Wilson disappeared from his work area at the dock. He was found hiding at the shoreline among some large rocks. When confronted with guards and guns, he surrendered.

SEPTEMBER 29, 1958

In September 1958, Clyde Johnson and Aaron Burgett, two inmates on garbage detail, assaulted a guard and tried to swim away. Johnson was recaptured in the water, but Burgett disappeared. Two weeks later, his body turned up floating in the bay.

DECEMBER 16, 1962

In mid-December 1962, two inmates bent out the protective bars from the kitchen window in the cell house basement and escaped. Darl Parker was recaptured on an outcropping of rock

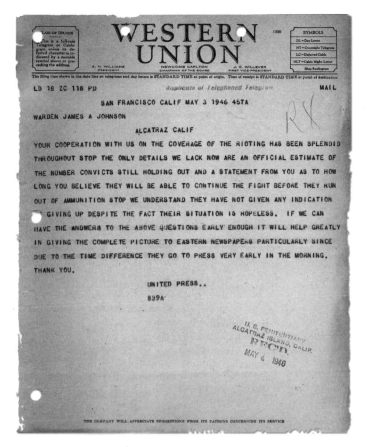

CLASS OF SERVICE		1220	SYMBOLS
This is a full-rate Telegram or Cable-gram unless its de-ferred character is in-dicated by a suitable symbol above or pre-ceding the address.	A. N. WILLIAMS PRESIDENT — NEWCOMB CARLTON CHAIRMAN OF THE BOARD — J. C. WILLEVER FIRST VICE-PRESIDENT		DL = Day Letter NT = Overnight Telegram LC = Deferred Cable NLT = Cable Night Letter Ship Radiogram

The filing time shown in the date line on telegrams and day letters is STANDARD TIME at point of origin. Time of receipt is STANDARD TIME at point of destination

LD 18 ZC 118 PD   Duplicate of Telephoned Telegram   MAIL

SAN FRANCISCO CALIF MAY 3 1946 457A

WARDEN JAMES A JOHNSON

ALCATRAZ CALIF

YOUR COOPERATION WITH US ON THE COVERAGE OF THE RIOTING HAS BEEN SPLENDID
THROUGHOUT STOP THE ONLY DETAILS WE LACK NOW ARE AN OFFICIAL ESTIMATE OF
THE NUMBER CONVICTS STILL HOLDING OUT AND A STATEMENT FROM YOU AS TO HOW
LONG YOU BELIEVE THEY WILL BE ABLE TO CONTINUE THE FIGHT BEFORE THEY RUN
OUT OF AMMUNITION STOP WE UNDERSTAND THEY HAVE NOT GIVEN ANY INDICATION
GIVING UP DESPITE THE FACT THEIR SITUATION IS HOPELESS. IF WE CAN
HAVE THE ANSWERS TO THE ABOVE QUESTIONS EARLY ENOUGH IT WILL HELP GREATLY
IN GIVING THE COMPLETE PICTURE TO EASTERN NEWSPAPERS PARTICULARLY SINCE
DUE TO THE TIME DIFFERENCE THEY GO TO PRESS VERY EARLY IN THE MORNING.
THANK YOU.

UNITED PRESS..

839A

U. S. PENITENTIARY
ALCATRAZ ISLAND, CALIF.
RECD.
MAY 4 1946

THE COMPANY WILL APPRECIATE SUGGESTIONS FROM ITS PATRONS CONCERNING ITS SERVICE

In this telegram from the 1946 Battle of Alcatraz, the United Press thanks Warden Johnston for keeping them up to date on the battle and asks for more information as it becomes available. (COURTESY NATIONAL PARK SERVICE, MUSEUM MANAGEMENT PROGRAM AND ALCATRAZ ISLAND, TELEGRAM TO WARDEN JOHNSTON FROM UNITED PRESS, GOGA 18308D, WWW.CR.NPS.GOV/MUSEUM)

in the bay, close to Alcatraz. John Paul Scott tried to swim toward the mainland but was caught in the swift, strong currents. He was found by a boatload of teenagers, shivering on a group of rocks under the Golden Gate Bridge, and was hospitalized briefly on the mainland before being sent back to the island.

5.

THE GREAT
ESCAPE

The only possibly successful escape from Alcatraz took place on June 11, 1962, and involved four men: Frank Lee Morris, Clarence and John Anglin, and Allen West.

The inmates were all men who had called little attention to themselves while in Alcatraz. Frank Morris, who had escaped from several other prisons during his long prison career and had come to Alcatraz in January 1960, worked in one of the prison shops, making brushes. There he had access to all kinds of materials and tools to aid in an escape. John Anglin worked in the clothing room in the prison basement, from which he gathered the materials needed to survive in the bay. Clarence Anglin worked in the prison barbershop, which allowed him to steal shorn hair, an essential part of the men's plan to elude the guards. Allen West worked on the painting crew in the utility corridor, where he saw the deterioration of the concrete walls, learned the geography of the utility area, and figured out how it could be accessed from the tiny air vents at the back of the prisoners' cells.

Although West always took credit for masterminding the 1962 break, it is more likely that Frank Morris, with his superior intelligence and long history of escaping from other prisons, was the one who actually planned the break and thought of every possible problem. Morris was cool and smart and did not have a history of violence. Unlike other attempted escapes, this plan did not rely on grabbing weapons or taking hostages. Rather, it was based on the well-known prison routine and the crumbling condition of the building

PREPARING THE ESCAPE

Phase one of the inmates' plan involved the use of a small utility shaft that lay behind the air vents in each man's cell. Through the shaft, the prisoners could climb to the top of the building and get out without being seen. But first the men had to reach the shaft, and to do that they needed to dig out the concrete in their cells. Luckily for them, the digging was made easier by the salt water that sloshed through the prison toilets. Over the years, the salt had corroded the cells' cement, making it easier to chip away.

Also working in the inmates' favor was the fact that each man had a cell next to that of another conspirator. The Anglins were in B-150 and B-152. Morris was in B-138, and West was in B-140. The prisoners began the work of chipping off the cement around their air vents at five-thiry each evening and continued until 9 P.M., just before the final head count and lights out. This was the largest block of time the men had in their cells every day, and each one took a turn looking out for guards while his partner dug.

As the wall came apart, each man took the pieces of chipped concrete from his cell, sprinkling them out of his pants as he walked around the yard during the daily recreation period. With the tunnel cleared, the men could navigate their way to the utility shaft and outside.

To be sure that each prisoner was accounted for, there were head counts twelve times a day at Alcatraz. The final head count of the evening was at 9 P.M., and there would not be another one until seven o'clock the next morning. By leaving at night, the men would have a ten-hour head start before they were missed. But guards continually patrolled the corridors looking for prisoners asleep in all the cells. To prevent suspicion, the Anglins constructed lifelike heads for each man to put under the cover of his cot as a decoy. The heads were covered with the hair Clarence Anglin had taken from the barbershop.

The prisoners were aware of the difficult conditions they would face once they reached the bay and had fashioned life jackets and a raft out of raincoats John Anglin had stolen from the clothing room. The jackets would protect them from both the currents and the cold. The life jackets and the raft were hidden in the Anglins' cells, along with a pump to blow up the raft, which Morris had made from a musical instrument he had stolen from the band room.

Previous escape attempts on Alcatraz had revolved around the idea of heading for the city of San Francisco, where the inmates could disappear among the city's hundreds of thousands of residents. The prisoners knew that the search for them would be concentrated there, and so they decided to head for nearby Angel Island instead. Reaching it would give them a chance to rest and keep them safe from the intense manhunt on the mainland that was sure to follow the news of their escape. When some of the heat had died down, they would go to the mainland, steal a car, and rob a clothing store in nearby Marin County for civilian suits and money. Then the men would go their separate ways. They had thought of everything, and finally the time had come to make their escape.

But as it turned out, West was not ready. Some months earlier, thinking that the guards were getting suspicious of them, West had filled in his partially dug hole with fresh plaster. Unfortunately, the plaster had hardened, making it much more difficult for him to chip it away. West urged Morris to go on without him, saying that he would catch up if he could.

One of the cells in Cell Block B that played a part in the great escape. The accordion case beneath the sink blocks the exit, and a fake head lies on the bed.
(© BETTMANN / CORBIS)

In the Anglins' cells, the two brothers moved silently through their tunnels, pushing the life jackets ahead of them. John Anglin also pushed the heavy folded bulk of the raft. They wriggled swiftly through the broken concrete and into the vertical utility shaft, where they met Morris.

The distance from the floor of the utility shaft to the metal grate set in the ceiling above their heads was over ten feet. Without help or a ladder of some sort, no one could reach the grate to open it. Working together, the men managed to scale the utility shaft, finally reaching the second floor.

The utility shaft was the same on each floor, and again the men helped one another up. Finally, Morris and the Anglin brothers climbed through the uppermost grate and onto the roof of the prison building, which was bathed in the glow of white searchlights from a tower at one end of the building. Staying close together and trying to avoid the lights, the men crept toward the drainpipe fixed in place on the side of the building. One by one, they climbed down until they reached a hill that led down to the cold waters of the bay.

They scrambled over the lip of the hill and then they made their way down the slope.

Unknown to them, Allen West, desperate to follow, had gone back to work in his cell. He had chipped away enough concrete around the vent to wriggle through and scrambled after them into the utility corridor, but it was now after 2 A.M., and the others were long gone.

West's one great chance to escape was also gone. Miserable, he returned to his cell, where neighboring prisoners could hear him sobbing.

THE MANHUNT IS ON

The next morning, head count started as usual at 7 A.M. All but three of the inmates stood facing out of their cells. The guards didn't understand why they were having trouble waking the last few prisoners until one of them impatiently reached through the bars of John Anglin's cell to shake his head.

The head bounced out of the bed and crashed onto the floor.

The guard leaped back three feet.

In less than fifteen minutes, the guards knew that the three inmates were missing. In his cell, Allen West held up the vent from his wall, which he'd painstakingly broken through, only to be left behind. He banged on it and said to the guards, "You may as well lock me up, too. I planned the entire escape!"

In a stroke of luck for the prisoners, the warden was not on the island at the time. His second in command, Acting Warden Art Dollison, was notified at his apartment on the island and hurried out the door just a few minutes after the sirens sounded. By 8 A.M., an all-points bulletin had been issued for the three men both on Alcatraz and in mainland California.

It didn't take long to determine how they had broken out. Moreover, it was clear that this was not a haphazard escape attempt. The cons had thought it all out. Obviously, they would be much more difficult to find than those who just tried to jump the wall or take hostages. The authorities brought in bloodhounds from San Quentin, which sniffed along the trail the three inmates had taken to the water's edge.

But the trail ended there.

In the first few days, the prison officials questioned thirty-eight prisoners who might have had knowledge of the plot. West, eager to show off and claim credit for the escape, talked freely, telling them that Morris and the Anglins were headed for Angel Island and explaining how they planned to get out of the area afterward. Officials found that the inmates' trail across Alcatraz led to the north part of the island, the right direction if they were indeed headed for Angel Island.

Officers investigating Angel Island found paddles in the water that looked like the ones that had been fashioned for the escape. They also discovered a waterproof bag made of raincoats floating between Alcatraz and Angel Island. Inside the bag they found a letter written to Clarence Anglin, photos of the Anglin family, and nine sheets of paper with contact names and information that West had included.

Obviously, the fugitives had headed for Angel Island.

But had they made it? There was no sign of them on the island, which was combed practically inch by inch. If they *had* reached the island alive, how had they gotten away from it? They had no friends or relatives who could come to rescue them. They had no money that could tempt strangers to help them and no way of contacting anyone, anyway. They all would have needed food, fresh clothes, and transportation to the mainland.

What is known is that the tide was running very fast and high on the night of June 11 at the time the three men would have taken to the water. It's easy to imagine that a rickety raft could lose air from a punctured side and the men would be thrown

A WEEK AFTER THE THREE MEN VANISHED, THE WARDEN RECEIVED A POSTCARD WRITTEN IN PENCIL, SAYING, "HA, HA, HA! WE MADE IT! FRANK, JOHN, AND CLARENCE."

into the water to fend for themselves. In the shoes and heavy Alcatraz-issue pea coats the prisoners wore against the cold weather, it would have been only a matter of minutes before they were saturated and pulled under.

Frank Morris, at five feet seven inches and only 135 pounds, was not muscular and easily could have been overwhelmed by such fast, cold water if he had tried to swim for it. The Anglins were beefier and better swimmers, but they still would have had to contend with the biting cold and the treacherous currents. And losing the bag filled with information they would need to survive on the mainland was indicative that in letting it go, they must have been desperate.

A week after the three men vanished, the warden received a postcard, saying, "Ha, ha, ha! We made it! Frank, John, and Clarence." The FBI determined that there were no fingerprints on it and that Clarence Anglin hadn't written it, but they could not decide whether Morris or John Anglin had done so.

At the same time, several phone calls started coming in to the attorney general's office in San Francisco from a man claiming to be John Anglin. A few days later, a man claiming to be Morris phoned Acting Warden Dollison, but when Dollison questioned him about personal details he was certain Morris would know, the man became vague and hung up.

Over the next few weeks, several items surfaced that supported the idea that the men had drowned. Two homemade life-jackets much like the one the three had left behind for West appeared at different times in the bay. Both had puncture marks, and when they were repaired and inflated, they lost almost all their air within an hour.

Then, on July 17, a seaman on a Norwegian ship spotted a body floating in the water about twenty miles west northwest of the Golden Gate Bridge. The seaman notified the ship's chief officer, who had to make a decision. The ship did not have a large cold-storage facility aboard; it could not take on a body. The two men both knew about the three inmates who had escaped from Alcatraz, and suspected this might be one of them. But they had no radio contact with the Coast Guard and could not notify anyone about it. Finally, the chief officer decided that they could not recover the body or take it back to the mainland. If it was one of the Alcatraz escapees, it meant the body had been floating for more than a month and would have been hideously disfigured.

The men noticed that the body had on "dirty" white trousers, which might have been the prisoners' blue denim, faded after being in the water so long. But that was all they saw, and they left the body behind. It was never found again.

Other Alcatraz inmates claimed that the three men couldn't have escaped successfully and then stayed underground. The Anglins talked too much to keep silent about their escapades, and Morris was unemployable and without a sufficient network of friends and relatives who would help him out.

Over the years, relatives of the Anglins claimed that strange beefy-looking and heavily veiled "women" had shown up at family funerals. Family members said that the women were John and Clarence in disguise. People who had known Morris years before claimed to have spotted him on the street years after the escape, but nothing ever came of any of those "leads."

Did the three men actually escape from Alcatraz? Or were they simply more victims of the freezing-cold bay tides who sank without a trace? No one knows for sure.

Allen West, who happily told everything he knew to the warden and guards, was immediately put into isolation as an accessory to the escape. His first act after being locked in the cell was to broadcast his story to all the other cons in isolation, speaking to them through the toilets. He bragged that even if he hadn't made it out with the others, he had ruined Alcatraz's escape-proof reputation. But there are many, including the warden, the inmates, and the FBI agents who questioned West at length, who think that what he said to Morris that night about not being able to get through the vent had been just an excuse. They believe that West, who had always shown a morbid fear of the water, lost his nerve at the last minute. Of course, his belated, futile attempt to catch up with the others and the realization that they'd left him might have saved his life.

West left the Rock in early 1963 for McNeil Island and then was transferred to Atlanta and finally to a series of state prisons, where he served time for other crimes. He was released for good in 1967, but he was a lifelong criminal and was soon back in prison for theft, robbery, and attempted escape. In December 1978, he complained of severe stomach pains and was sent to the hospital. He died there on December 21 at the age of forty-nine.

To the end of his life, West bragged that he and the three men who never returned had broken the Rock. Whether that was true or not, the 1962 escape certainly hastened the closing of America's toughest prison.

THE PRISON DOOR
6. CLOSES

On March 21, 1963, the federal penitentiary on Alcatraz was closed forever.

There were many factors in the decision to shut it down. To begin with, times had changed. Alcatraz had opened during an era with an unusually high rate of violent crime and notorious gangsters. Removing the worst criminals to a secluded community where they could be kept under intense scrutiny day and night was considered a good idea.

But in the early 1960s the criminals were different. No longer were national figures with familiar faces making their way down Broadway. The new criminals were usually unknown to their fellow prisoners and were usually there for an average of five years, some of them having come directly from a courtroom rather than being sent to Alcatraz because of bad behavior in another prison.

In addition, prison reformers had become concerned with rehabilitating convicts and preparing them for life outside prison. Alcatraz had no way to help prisoners adjust to a new life. It was concerned only with keeping them isolated.

More important, Alcatraz was no longer impossible to escape from. The great escape of 1962 had proved that its security was no longer foolproof, and keeping the most dangerous prisoners

ALCATRAZ WAS NO LONGER IMPOSSIBLE TO ESCAPE FROM. THE GREAT ESCAPE OF 1962 HAD PROVED THAT ITS SECURITY WAS NO LONGER FOOLPROOF, AND KEEPING THE MOST DANGEROUS PRISONERS LOCKED AWAY TOGETHER IN ONE PLACE, NO MATTER HOW ISOLATED, SUDDENLY NO LONGER SEEMED A GOOD IDEA.

locked away together in one place, no matter how isolated, suddenly no longer seemed a good idea.

The physical layout of the prison also contributed to the demise of Alcatraz. Years of salt water in the plumbing had corroded the pipes and helped crumble the concrete of the prison building. Contractors calculated the cost of repairing the buildings at more than $5 million.

The Justice Department might have been willing to pay for the renovation if it had not also looked at the costs of running the prison. Alcatraz had the smallest prisoner population of any federal penitentiary, with the highest ratio of guards to prisoners. That ratio was a large part of the reason Alcatraz had remained so secure for so many years. But that kind of security cost money.

When it was revealed that it cost $10.10 per day to keep a prisoner on Alcatraz, whereas housing the same prisoner cost $3 per day in Atlanta, Attorney General Robert F. Kennedy decided there was no further need for the Rock. There were too few prisoners, and too much money was being spent to justify the price it would cost to restore Alcatraz to its former efficiency.

Kennedy called for the closing of the prison and the transfer of all remaining inmates to other federal prisons on the U.S. mainland. In October 1962, the first prisoners were airlifted off the island and transferred to other prisons. A few months later, the last and most difficult prisoners were taken off the island, and the facility was shut down for good

At the time of the June 1962 breakout, there had been over 330 inmates. Nine months later, Alcatraz was deserted. It would never be used as a prison again.

"THE INDIANS HAVE LANDED!"

7.

A FIRST ATTEMPT

By 1968, American Indians living in the Bay Area were beginning to feel desperate for a home. They wanted to find a place that would give them decent housing, work, and an education for their children while preserving their culture. They thought Alcatraz might be the place.

Here was a piece of land that was still abandoned six years after its prison doors had closed for good. It could be a symbol of Native American pride. It could house Indians on their own land. It could be home to an Indian museum, learning center, and cultural area. It could provide jobs through a plant that would remove salt from the water of the bay.

The United Council, which represented all the tribes in the Bay Area, began to talk about ways to achieve their goals. They wrote a proclamation to explain their message and their hopes for a new kind of Indian pride, which would be embodied in Alcatraz. They decided to take the island back on November 9. It was a slow time for news, and they believed they would get more press attention at that point.

The United Council chartered boats for its members to get across the bay and contacted their friends in the local media.

They announced that the Indians were claiming Alcatraz and asked for press coverage.

But on November 9, none of the chartered boats appeared at the dock where they were supposed to be. The members of the United Council, feeling desperate, asked others to come, but they did not appear, either. Then they saw a man on a boat in the

THE FIRST LANDING

On March 8, 1964, almost a year to the day after Alcatraz was closed as a prison, five Sioux tribal members and their lawyer, along with members of the local Indian council and a group of curious reporters, landed on the island. The Sioux were wearing full Indian tribal gear, including feathered headdresses and beads. They came without weapons but carrying a proclamation. They had come, they said, to stake a claim to the land under an 1868 treaty between the United States government and the Indians.

Their attorney explained to the island's caretaker that under the 1868 treaty, the United States had granted any members of the Sioux tribe who did not live on an Indian reservation the right to claim any land that the government had once owned for a fortress or another military use and then abandoned. Alcatraz clearly fit into that category.

The five Sioux were not interested in stealing the land. The United States government had recently offered to pay 47 cents an acre to California Indians whose land had been taken since 1849. The Sioux told reporters that they would pay the same 47 cents an acre to buy Alcatraz, or $9.40 for the whole island. And if it didn't interfere with the Indians' homestead, they would allow the government to keep the lighthouse on the island, as they realized it was a safety measure for ships in the bay.

By that time, the acting warden, Richard Willard, had arrived from the mainland. He told the party that they were trespassing on government land and ordered them to leave immediately. Their lawyer advised them to go, saying that they had made their point, and the Sioux packed up their gear and left quietly.

The "occupation" lasted only four hours. The next day, local newspapers called it a crazy stunt. The five Sioux never did buy the land or try to live on it again. The incident was forgotten almost immediately.

A group of Souix tribal members protest at Alcatraz in an attempt to claim the land under a 1868 treaty with the U.S. government. (© BETTMANN/CORBIS)

bay. He was friendly and interested in their cause. The captain explained to the head of the council that he could not pull up at the dock on Alcatraz because the keel of his boat rode too low in the water. But he would take them around the island so that they could see it and bring them back to the mainland. The Indians agreed. It was better than nothing, and they were disappointed and frustrated that their plans were not working out.

As the boat neared Alcatraz, several American Indians could not resist the temptation to set foot on land. They threw themselves into the chilly water and paddled frantically for the Rock.

The captain was horrified. His boat flew the Canadian flag, and if passengers from his vessel attempted to reach land illegally, that could be interpreted by the U.S. government as an act of war by Canada against the United States. He pleaded with the head of the council to talk to his people and order them not to swim toward the island.

Of the four Native Americans who had jumped overboard, one reached Alcatraz safely. He stayed on it only long enough to grin and dance around. The others were picked up, still in the water, by other boats in the area and returned to the mainland.

A NIGHTTIME CROSSING

The next evening, during a quiet night crossing, fourteen Indians managed to get onto the island with sleeping bags and supplies. There were others on the boat, but the captain, who had been hired by the Indians to take them to the island without being told why, panicked when he was told the Native Americans were going to stay. He was certain the Coast Guard would hold him responsible and take his boat away, and so he pulled away from the dock before the rest of the group had stepped down. Also left on the boat were many of the Indians' supplies.

The island was overseen at that time by a caretaker named John Hart, a former prison guard. Hart and a group from the Coast Guard set off in search of the Indians, who were well outnumbered. The Indians stayed out of sight until they realized that they probably could not hold out without weapons or manpower for much longer. Then they trooped out of their hiding places, came down to the dock, and read aloud their proclamation, which explained in detail their reasons for occupying Alcatraz and what they hoped to accomplish. It was signed "Indians of All Tribes."

The Native Americans were told to leave at once or face trespassing charges. Their leader, Richard Oakes, replied that the Indians had established squatter's rights—the right to claim ownership of the land because they were already physically there—and would return.

They did. On November 20, only ten days later, a group of ninety American Indians landed on Alcatraz in the middle of the night. John Hart, the caretaker, had gone fishing in the mountains but had left an assistant in his place. The assistant woke up when he heard the noise outside, saw the landing, and shouted, "Mayday! Mayday! The Indians have landed!"

By four o'clock that day, government officials were on the island, insisting that the Indians leave.

The Indians did not resist, but they also did not leave. Instead, they remained for nineteen remarkable months.

LIFE ON ALCATRAZ

For the first three days after the arrival of the Native Americans on Alcatraz, the Coast Guard tried to blockade the island, using its cutters to prevent supplies from reaching the Indians and thus forcing them to leave.

Soon, however, the press picked up the story, and support began to stream in from all over the country. Everyone, it seemed, from Hollywood celebrities to ordinary people who felt picked on themselves, could relate to the Indians' desire for a place where they could live and be free. Those supporters sent both money and supplies, and daring captains around the bay used small, fast boats to run the supplies out to Alcatraz.

The Indians, it seemed, were there to stay.

Once the Native Americans had settled in, a number of important innovations occurred, beginning with the opening of the Big Rock School, an Indian school on the island that taught children about their heritage and customs as well as academic subjects. Since for many years the government had tried to keep Indian children ignorant of those customs, tearing them away from their heritage, the Indians considered this a critical part of their program on Alcatraz.

The Native Americans also opened an arts center, a health clinic, and a kitchen to cook community meals and took on the work of repairing the old facilities so that they could live there comfortably. Upon arriving on Alcatraz, they discovered that there were only three working toilets on the entire island. Within a few weeks, the Native American who worked as their plumber had raised that number to thirty-five.

THANKSGIVING ON ALCATRAZ

The first major event the Indians celebrated on Alcatraz—only one week after they had taken the island—was Thanksgiving. Hundreds of Indians from the mainland came out by boat to take part in the celebration as well. When they reached the dock at Alcatraz, a Native American security guard met them with the words "Welcome to Alcatraz! You are now on Indian land."

Ironically, one of the people who came to celebrate Thanksgiving on the island was Alice Carnes, the mother of Clarence Carnes, the Choctaw Indian who had been part of the 1946 Battle of Alcatraz and who remained a prisoner on the island until 1963.

The Thanksgiving feast celebrated in 1969 was the most glorious moment for the Native American movement on Alcatraz. In the next few weeks, the Indians would begin to realize a number of their long-held dreams.

Most of the single young men moved into cells in the old prison building. Couples who had brought their children chose the old residential complex at the far end of the island where the guards and their families had lived. Visitors also stayed in that area when they came to the island. And in the first few months there were many visitors. A lot of people, Indian and non-Indian, wanted to see what the Indians would make of Alcatraz.

But soon the Native Americans began to argue. Although they all shared the work of the island, they disagreed on how Alcatraz should be run. The unity that had made occupation possible in the first place began to splinter. At the same time, a charismatic young student leader named Richard Oakes—the same man who had claimed squatting rights for the Indians—began a campaign stating that the Native Americans on Alcatraz, not those staying on the mainland, should decide how to run the island.

This angered the members of the United Council, who felt that without their initial leadership and continual pleas to supporters and the press, the Indians on Alcatraz would have had nothing. Since everything on Alcatraz had to be brought there by boat and so much depended on the goodwill and support of outsiders, the council felt that Oakes and those who agreed with him were ungrateful and arrogant. But the United Council had another problem that would eventually be the undoing of the Indians on Alcatraz.

BAD PRESS COMES TO ALCATRAZ

As time passed, drugs and alcohol found their way onto the island. Fights broke out over the new "supplies," and the peaceful existence of the island's occupants was threatened. The United Council tried to see things in a positive light. They told themselves that when people saw what was happening on Alcatraz, they would realize that this was how Indians had lived on reservations for generations and sympathize even more with their problems.

But that was not what happened.

Instead, many previously enthusiastic supporters withdrew their support. They had seen Alcatraz as a place to realize Native American ideals, not to show how badly Indians could behave. They felt they could not continue to send money or supplies to support the occupants' self-destructive behavior.

When reports of the Indians' behavior began to appear in the local newspapers, the Indians became insulted. They saw any

RICHARD OAKES

At the time that he spoke out against mainlanders running Alcatraz, Richard Oakes was just twenty-seven years old, ordinarily too young to be considered a leader in the Native American tradition. But he previously had been president of the Indian students at San Francisco State University, and he lived on the island with his family. He was handsome, forceful, and passionate about the occupation and what the Native Americans intended to accomplish there. Not surprisingly, he was much quoted by the press, and the occupiers looked to him for inspiration and leadership.

Two months after the occupation began, however, Richard's adopted daughter, Yvonne, fell down three flights in the officers' quarters. Though they got her to a mainland hospital at once, she died.

Richard and his wife, Ann, were crushed. Eventually his grief caused him to be so disruptive and argumentative that the Indians on the island insisted that he leave. He and his family left Alcatraz for good shortly afterward.

Richard's life off Alcatraz featured a number of bizarre confrontations. In 1972, he found himself in an argument in northern California, siding with a few Indian boys against police officers. The boys had taken horses belonging to the local YMCA camp and were riding them. The officers tried to stop them, and the argument rapidly got out of hand.

Richard tried to calm down both sides. The police saw him reach toward his jacket. Though he was unarmed, one officer thought he intended to draw a weapon and fired, killing him. He was thirty-one years old.

criticism of their island life, no matter how justified, as intolerable and sent away any reporter who wrote an unfavorable story. Inevitably, press support for the occupation began to erode, and with it much of the power of the Native Americans to keep the land.

THE END OF THE OCCUPATION

With island life deteriorating, the government began to work even harder to get the Native Americans off Alcatraz. They began by offering them land elsewhere but eventually resorted to other methods. The government towed away the barge that brought a quarter million gallons of fresh water to the island every week. Without it, the Indians had to bring in water by hand in five-gallon containers. Then they took away electrical power, but the Indians hooked their own generator up to the old lighthouse and restored power.

But on June 1, 1970, something happened that the Indians could not ignore. Around ten o'clock in the evening, they realized that the island was on fire.

There was no spare water, and the buildings that were blazing were old and wooden, including the recreation hall and the warden's house. Since they had no updated firefighting equipment, the Indians immediately started a bucket brigade. One person at the end of a line of people filled buckets full of water and passed them down the line. The last person to receive the buckets—the person who was closest to the fire—threw the water on the flames. But it was not enough to stop the fire. There was little the Indians could do but watch it take down everything it touched. It even took out the light in the

A man stands outside a tepee pitched on the island during the American Indian Movement takeover of Alcatraz. (© BETTMANN/CORBIS)

An American Indian girl—one of the 78 who invaded Alcatraz Island— paints "Indian American Land" on the wall of a former prison building. (© BETTMANN/CORBIS)

lighthouse, which had been a safety beacon in the bay since the nineteenth century.

Finally, on June 11, 1971—nineteen months after the Indians of All Tribes had claimed Alcatraz as their own—three Coast Guard cutters arrived on the island. They carried thirty armed federal marshals and Coast Guard personnel, who surrounded the island and took the residents off against their will. At that time there were only fifteen people on the island: six men, four women, and five children. The others who lived on Alcatraz were on the mainland collecting supplies and doing errands.

They would never be allowed back on the island. The Indians were taken to the nearby Coast Guard station on Yerba Buena Island, questioned, and searched. After a late lunch, they were taken by launch to San Francisco.

The great American Indian occupation of Alcatraz was over.

But it had served a purpose. As a result of the occupation, the U.S. government gave up its long standing policy of separating Native Americans from their cultural customs and groups and agreed to allow them to keep their cultural identity. The Indians might have lost the battle to keep Alcatraz, but they won an important victory.

8. ALCATRAZ TODAY

In 1972, the United States Congress created the Golden Gate National Recreation Area, setting aside many acres of land in California for the enjoyment of the public. Strangely, the twenty-acre barren island out in the bay was included. The place where no one ever wanted to go would now become an area where, if they wished, all people could go. Alcatraz became a protected area that could be used both as an ecological preserve and as a tourist attraction. The island—which was opened to the public in 1973 and immediately drew an enthusiastic response and tens of thousands of visitors—quickly became one of the most popular tourist attractions in the country. Everyone, it seemed, wanted to come to Alcatraz.

Today, more than a million visitors a year travel by ferry to the barren little island in the middle of the bay. Some pay as much as $69 a ticket for admission. The National Park Service offers several types of tours, including special night programs on every subject from the Civil War dungeons to Al Capone to the every-day life of both the prisoners and the residents while it was a federal prison.

Upon arriving on the island, visitors gather around eagerly as National Park Service rangers talk about the history of the island. They ask questions about the American Indian occupation in the late 1960s and about Alcatraz's current status as a preserve for one of the largest seagull colonies in northern California.

But it seems that nothing fascinates visitors more than the stories of Alcatraz's time as a federal prison. Guests are invited to walk through the old prison buildings and poke around the cell where Al Capone spent much of his time forty years before. They may even try to talk to one another through the toilet bowls in each cell, as prisoners once did. In the mess hall, visitors can look at the board that lists the last meal ever served to prisoners. They are also encouraged to examine D block, the isolation area, before being closed into the Strip Cell by a tour guide. And of course, they ask about the famous escape attempts.

Occasionally, the tour guides are actually former prisoners, who answer questions from visitors and try to explain to them what it was like to live on the island.

To add to the eerie atmosphere, over the years a number of prisoners, guards, and modern-day tour guides have claimed to hear sounds or see apparitions around the island, particularly in the area of the prison building.

Prison guards also claim to have heard strange noises and even to have smelled smoke that convinced them the prison laundry was on fire. But when they checked it out, there was no fire and no apparent cause for the smell.

Today's tour guides often report hearing the sounds of sobbing as they make the rounds of empty rooms and cells. One tour guide claimed to hear the sound of banjo music coming from the empty shower room. It was the same shower room

A HAUNTING AT ALCATRAZ?

As early as the 1940s, prisoners were claiming to see or hear strange things. A prisoner sent to the Hole for breaking the rules began to scream within a few minutes of being locked in and claimed that something with glowing eyes was staring at him. The guards laughed at him, but when they returned in the morning, he was dead—his face frozen in horror. Even stranger, he had been strangled, and not by his own hand.

To add to the strangeness, when they did a head count that morning, there was one more prisoner than was supposed to be there. When they looked closely at the prisoners' faces, they saw the prisoner whose dead body they had just found! He stared at them and then vanished.

This view of "Broadway" remains as prisoners would have seen it when they first arrived on the island. (COURTESY NATIONAL PARK SERVICE, MUSEUM MANAGEMENT PROGRAM AND ALCATRAZ ISLAND, BROADWAY, WWW.CR.NPS.GOV/MUSEUM)

where a frightened Al Capone, his mind deteriorating with disease, used to hide rather than walk in the recreation yard. And of course, Capone did play the banjo.

No one can be certain what the sounds mean, where they come from, or whether they're real. But if it's true that ghosts return to the places where they suffered the most in life, Alcatraz would certainly be a natural place to harbor them.

Today's visitors enjoy hearing these stories and seeing the sights when they go to Alcatraz, but most leave with relief. It is fascinating, it is a little frightening, it has a colorful and exciting history.

But no one really wants to stay.

Even the gulls don't often stay on Alcatraz. They may stop for a few minutes to rest, but soon they are wheeling high over the island, making the same harsh cries heard by the prisoners long ago, day after endless day, year after endless year.

Alcatraz has served its purpose.

Now only the memories are left.

CHAPTER NOTES

The following notes consist of citations to the sources of quoted material. Each citation includes the first and last words or phrases of the quotation, and its source. References are to works cited in the Selected Bibliography, on the facing page.

Abbreviations used are:

AH—AlcatrazHistory.com

Babyak—*Breaking the Rock: The Great Escape from Alcatraz*

Eagle—*Alcatraz! Alcatraz! The Indian Occupation of Alcatraz*

Chapter Three: Famous Prisoners

PAGE

24   "Well, Warden ... licked": AH

25   "G-men ... shoot": AH

Chapter Five: The Great Escape

PAGE

54   "You may as well ... escape": Babyak, p. 219

57   "Ha! Ha! Ha! ... Clarence": Babyak, p. 232

Chapter Seven: The Indians Have Landed

PAGE

69   "Mayday! ... landed": Eagle, p. 73

71   "Welcome ... Indian land": Eagle, p. 83

BOOKS

Babyak, Jolene. *Breaking the Rock: The Great Escape from Alcatraz*. Berkeley, CA: Ariel Vamp Press, 2001.

————. *Eyewitness on Alcatraz: Life on The Rock as Told by the Guards, Families & Prisoners*. Berkeley, CA: Ariel Vamp Press, 1988.

Eagle, Adam Fortunate. *Alcatraz! Alcatraz! The Indian Occupation of 1969–1971*. Berkeley, CA: Heyday Books, 1992.

Godwin, John. *Alcatraz: 1868–1963*. Garden City, NY: Doubleday, 1963.

WEB SITES

www.AlcatrazHistory.com

www.AlcatrazTickets.com

www.nps.gov/alcatraz (official Park Services Web site)

INDEX